Loving
and
Laughing
during a
Pandemic

Sheri Horton

Archway Publishing books may be ordered through booksellers or by contacting:

Archway Publishing
1663 Liberty Drive
Bloomington, IN 47403
www.archwaypublishing.com
844-669-3957

ISBN: 978-1-6657-0049-8 (sc)
ISBN: 978-1-6657-0050-4 (hc)
ISBN: 978-1-6657-0048-1 (e)

Library of Congress Control Number: 2020925229

Print information available on the last page.

Archway Publishing rev. date: 10/20/2021

ARCHWAY
PUBLISHING

Loving
and
Laughing
during a
Pandemic

COVID prep

quickly assembled
toilet paper soars sky-high
unknown seas ahead

Face mask

accessory new
cute cuddles nestled safely
beautiful face ahh

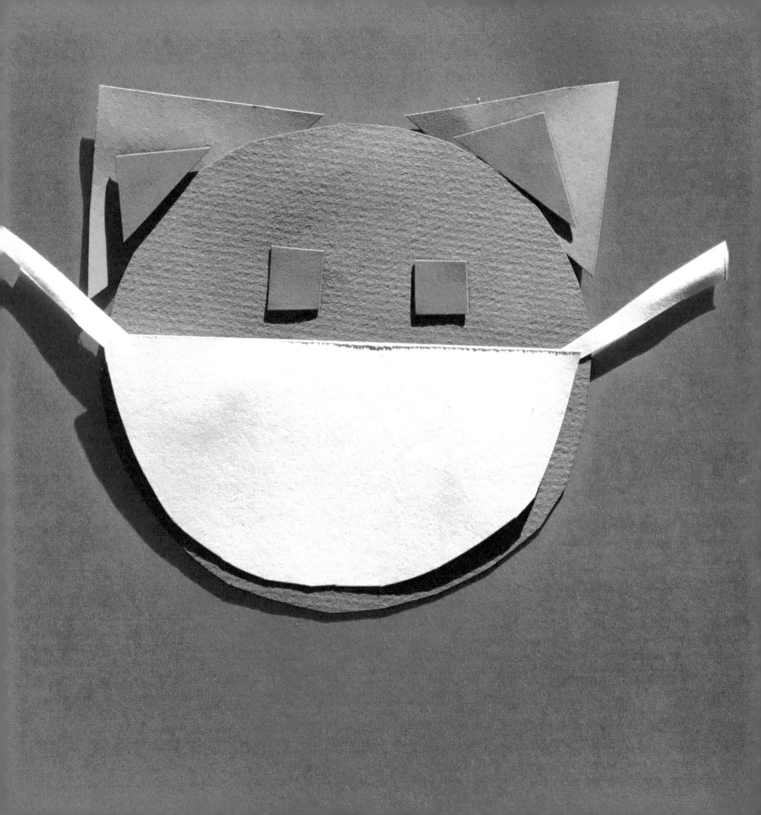

Line dancing

air kick ball change high
slide step cheek to cheek slip out
fresh clap turn stomp hop

Screen meeting

gridded colleagues smile
home turf calm nerves
fridge food numb
clean brain storm type board

We wear masks

soft clean delicate
we mask kind we mask cool we
ear loops love sweet style

Who is it?

masked robber boo
customer face covered nice
masked teller safe

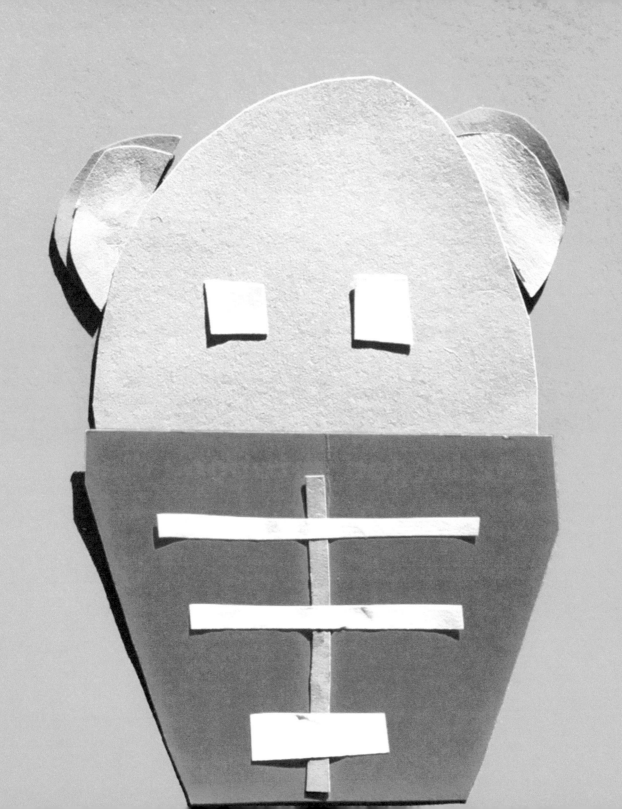

Dream office

warm palm tree delight
fringed blanket cool crisp sand
unplugged notebook glee

Fencing fun

double mask surprise
lunge advanced social distance
pitter patter swish

Shopping trip

store floor bold game board
plastic shinny living play
roll dice move you six

Diploma

sweet day dark tires squeal
families roll soar cry joy sigh
school pride up drop high

Kissing love

soft sweet strong sexy
mask cover soulful bright smile
anticipation

Snorkeling

rippled sandbar soothe
colorful schooled fish swim
cleaning coral reef

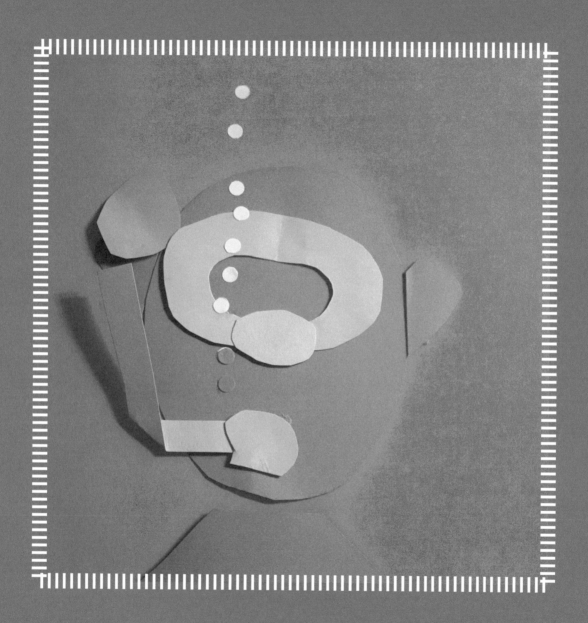

Please swim under lifeguard supervision.

Pal picnic

sunny cloud splinter
beyond fist bump distance yes
mending distant hearts

ID check

bare chilly shy face
flash smile camera snap pow
cradle face cloth zip

Pool closed

warm pool cool water
sunlight summer laughing bliss
now vertical swim

Please swim under lifeguard supervision

Author Biograph

Sheri loves travel, art and the water. She can be found laughing with her friends in person and via video.

Printed in the United States
by Baker & Taylor Publisher Services